Poetry Rhymes Tells a Story

82 New Poems

Poetry Rhymes Tells a Story

82 New Poems

An Eagle Falcon Publication

By

Dalward J DeBruzzi

E-BookTime, LLC
Montgomery, Alabama

Poetry Rhymes Tells a Story
82 New Poems

Library of Congress Control Number: 2019908386

ISBN: 978-1-60862-761-5

First Edition
Published August 2019
E-BookTime, LLC
6598 Pumpkin Road
Montgomery, AL 36108
www.e-booktime.com

A Casual Stroll

One day passed trees flower beds to a bird
fountain bath
Orioles, blue birds, red cardinals were
dipping for water
Playfully splashing, refreshed taking flight
without falter

Lovely colored autumn leaves on ground
wafting fluttering in air
Tuneful semi conscious lullaby restful
peaceful prayer

Caterpillars, cocoons beautiful butterfly
arise
Observing colorful beauty vibrant
enchanting surprise

Their breathless essence with eager ease
can abide
Stunning effect on senses will never
subside

Tall powerful oak tree amid dense wood
Majestic magnificence breathless understood

Few steps further sun shines on green hill
Traipsing with pleasure enjoyment still

Awe savory expectations orchard in view
Apples, pears, peaches prime tasty ready to chew

Meandering on over the valley towards sea shoal
As sun lowered concluded my restful casual stroll

by Dalward J DeBruzzi

A Feeling

An evening he was strolling in the fresh night air
Encountered a fair maiden with golden hair

Pining for the charitable courtesy for her to sit awhile
She disdained the offer with artifices and guile

Then she spoke with frank candid honesty
Inane pointless intimacy can cloud my chastity

I politely pointed out this was not a pitch to matrimony
She replied directly nor is it in the realm of sanctimony

Rationalized rejection because maiden devoid of taste
Labeled her impetuous and erroneous in her haste

Continued evening strolls but no pleasant surprises yet
Still have hope will find the girl should be met

by Dalward J DeBruzzi

A Mariner's Thoughts

**Been a sailor since skinny green lad of
sixteen
Traveled world over not many lands haven't
seen**

**Attracted by vastness exotic places thrilling
and new
Salty brine ports far and near exciting Peru
and Cebu**

**Love the waves steady lolling when smooth
and pacific
When King Triton behaving weather terrific**

**Oceans earn my praise can flee land for the
sea
Oh wind in my hair feet on rolling deck
vastness the key**

**With amassed experience and enhanced
reputation
Became 2nd officer on most famous liner of
creation**

Strutted proudly on deck now somewhat in
smug elation
Amid band fanfare speeches plaudits for
liner unequaled in expectation

Sailed with pomp great prophecies of
records salutation
Obsessed with speed reckless enhance
acclamation

Voyage a disaster a cold watery grave for
thousands in icy waters all terrified
and frantic
I was a sailing fanatic major failure in
judgment was on the Titanic

by Dalward J DeBruzzi

Acceptance

No scalpel or knife cuts as clean as a
rejecting sneer
Direct to the heart deep painful an
embarrassed smear

Finest of all sutures is a long passionate kiss
Formula for entering delightful throbbing bliss

How to acquire the persona to be really
wanted
Shed obnoxious behavior add pleasing ways
undaunted

Being rejected not selected akin to infection
Failure to adjust and improve you encourage
rejection

Gaining approval is an ubiquitous global
quest
Passing into desirable demand how blessed

Yet the stars have not dealt me as bad as they could do
My pleasures in life limited my serious troubles few

by Dalward J DeBruzzi

All's Well that Ends Well

Come sit down my sweet I've something to say
It's long on my mind for many a day

I'm not reckless nor a fool or a sot
I disavow and disdain the pipe and pot

Oh my sweetest this surely should be
You have so affected a young man as me

It's given I find myself able your wants to supply
Obstacles impediments to our course we decry

My case I plead am a man trusty and kind
In maiden's quest a favorable find

I come to thee on wings of love devotion and truth
A profound devout enraptured youth

All this laid at your feet for the taking
Renders both stricken an unbelievable
shaking

From the world's circumspect glaring eye
Observed a passion destined nare to die

She made vows agreed to surrender her
virginity
Only after the wedding nuptials satisfying
her dignity

by Dalward J DeBruzzi

Always

**Away back when two youngsters started
out lovers
Smooth then rocky road rough seas love
smothers**

**Then rediscovers values reconciliation
loomed
As years proceeded bond reseeded revived
love bloomed**

**Lived a placid entrancing life heaven hath
groomed
Filled with joy redundant good times and
thrills resumed**

**Our time now getting late in the day
One of us heaven bound at any time drifting
away**

**The departure no pleasure no selection
can't remain
Parting painful anguish heart strings
difficult sustain**

Love you yet though gracing the heavens
entranced
Near end myself soon you'll again be
romanced

Traveling life's path together was enriching
aflame
Pity to those who failed to achieve glorious
same

You're on my mind when I sit alone awake
At night wondering your welfare my heart in
dire ache

All is now redundant can recommence our
love affair
Can spend eternity together as planned long
ago with care

by Dalward J DeBruzzi

An Honest Woman

Old woman in shapeless attire in grey
Graced with lovely daughter charming and gay
Deception by chance willingly led astray

Glib false counterfeit fluttering tongue
Oaths promises unfaithfully sung

Romped in green fields meadows by streams
Hoping anointed reverence to realize dreams

Soon began to eruct in early morn
Mother crushed fears lovely daughter's innocence shorn

Who has violated my lovely daughter cried mama aloud
It was Roger Dodger who cajoled me then had me cowed

Mother ranted howled get my glasses and crutches anon
She faced, condemned him, the deed laid upon

She roared and screamed the truth you cannot deny fact

He replied I stand firm will share my house and land
Will take her for wife to enrich our life so grand

All's well that ends well when true hearts prevail
Mother's accented perspective at times needed for vessel to sail

by Dalward J DeBruzzi

Beauty Is Universal

Tis not the complexion that causes affection
What then influences the ultimate selection?
Thin nose, full lips, unblemished skin and graceful
Shapely figure, fine tapering thighs, demeanor tasteful
Fine bosom lovely eyes, evokes panting sighs
Elements that are possessed to qualify as a beauty
Present in all humanity where ever found a surety
Tis not the complexion that causes affection it's the body
My name is Song Lou I am almond eyed of the yellow race
I am fortuitous said attractive, sought after in chase
Most men want me like me way I look white men, Asians black men too
Tis not the complexion that causes affection it's the body

My name is Latanya Doleay I am a beauty contest winner beautiful in every way
I possess a lovely face and body that attracts men my way
My skin dark rich and shiny accenting my appeal each day
Tis not the complexion that causes affection it's the body
My name Sheila Gaines am pursued by men with intent
Body and figure a magnet to all men an ongoing event
Same problem every attractive girl puts up with
Tis not the complexion that causes affection it's the body

by Dalward J DeBruzzi

Behavioral Changes?

We were long acquainted thought I knew
her ways
Was just a lad knew her in happier days

True happiness is not in the number of
friends
But in the quality and direction of their
moral trends

Love mankind but women more with intense
passion
Adoration of females my abiding fashion

When surrendering my mortality don't grieve
for me
My life rich thanks to women, calm placid
as smooth sea

How many can say lived satisfied happy and
contentedly
This is the objective of what the good life
was meant to be

We were long acquainted thought I knew her ways
Was just a lad knew her in happier days

What I was deceived then wouldn't work now
Once conceded her beauteous tribute to thou

Once saw worth and character firm and strong
After behavioral change for worse deserted farewell and so long

by Dalward J DeBruzzi

Bird of Prey

In the mountainous Teton country its vast
domain
Hawk gliding hungrily wishing find prey to
sustain

Riding the wind with spiraling soaring flight
Circling swooping to find rodent, pheasant a
tasty bite
Mice, Pikas, fledgling fowl any a delightful
sight

Weasels and hawks compete for same prey
Beating them to dinner always a good day

Pocket gopher popped his head above
ground
Espied by hawk and weasel same time

Weasel leaped gripped pocket gopher no
instant to spare
Hawk finished dive came up with thin air
Both hawk and weasel irresponsible and
unfair

Gopher is a farmer plows up deep soil with
hundreds of tunnels aerates with toil
Despite grave danger he performs his task
true and loyal
Providing avoid hawk and weasel their
intensions foil

by Dalward J DeBruzzi

Blessed

Her simplicity, goodness, pure spirit won
me from the start
I thought of my prior gloom, an ennui that
formerly plagued my vacuous heart

Nature has no beauty fairer than thy
unbeguiled face
Warm sunshine of your heart encompassing
me is my bountiful grace

A lovelier nymph a pen or brush never drew
With substance your true mystic essence
sparkles, shining through

Soft gracious thoughts wordless meaning
plainly though subtle opaque purview
Caresses of love feelings senses grew

Catalyst needed to inflame binding
emotions of two
Body urges and spiritual commitment origin
of deep flourishing emotion

From this seed deep love can thrive, expand burgeon nourishing
Feel warm and excited when studying your face, bosom, derriere and bask in your presence

Am fulfilled when in your company a divine sensation
A feeling produced in no other company or situation

These words have been describing what true love is about
If you're a blessed one you have reason to boast and shout

by Dalward J DeBruzzi

Bossie Our Cow

She goes moo! is black and white
Love drinking her milk at breakfast, supper and night

She toils daily with untiring dedication no compensation
Requires no accolades praise, or needed motivation
Faithful in her production with eager participation

Scans the pasture for flowers and grass or nibbles some hay in the barn
Never sick, always healthy never causes alarm

Her pay is inadequate she ignores the discretion
Production not pay is her loyal intention

Each day what is not consumed by family is saved and stored in milk cans picked up by creamery truck
Creamery workers, truck driver love Bossie too for their employment and good luck

With this marvelous animal there is still more to be stated
Besides all amazing things we can say Bossie is under rated

At the end of every month the creamery sends us a check as payment
This wonderful animal provides us steady income yet never a claimant

Were blessed with this marvelous soul
Unanimously elected "THE QUEEN" in a family poll

by Dalward J DeBruzzi

Captive Visions

Sweet adored nymph that liv’st unseen
thoughts only
Spring is come the flowers burst to bloom
some lonely

Seeds of flower burst bloom radiate in
splendor then demise
Floating visions of svelte beauteous nymph
remains personal prize

Tis tender love true souls will hope to nourish
bequeath
Some endure some abort this asunder my
nymph beneath

Diaphanous visions persistent in my senses
Pleasure unlimited no boundaries confining
fences

Sweet adored nymph that liv’st unseen
thoughts only
Enriches with wild imagination free license
nevermore lonely

by Dalward J DeBruzzi

Comic Opera

I will squander no time with enmity
It corrodes, rots more destructive than absent sobriety

Instead spent my time pursuing happiness with domesticity for me
The quest was noble the unfolding drama a tragic decree

My first wife a sweet charming girl with a weakness at table
She grew to ponderous proportions as, in a fable

My second wife said she adored me was agreeable
Developed a razor sharp deadly tongue not foreseeable

Third wife swore to honor and obey be a true mate
Found by accident was often with our plumber on a date

Fourth wife a dedicated nurse in immaculate white
Took care of me with medical skills day and night

Thought finally was fortuitous could relax, composed
Feigned happy and content but really indisposed

One morning left a note
She fled with a doctor issued summons left me blue

My luck ran deep and steady but lamentable
All bad painful grievous and regrettable
Found affection, loyalty, devotion my choice not debatable

A fine spritely spirited Irish setter
On my oath I found contentment my life is better

People asked is this pet your first dog we implore?
No I say without animosity, I've had four before

by Dalward J DeBruzzi

Confessions

I am not free of defects I must confess
But whose perfect more or less

I mean not to defend my flaws though many
Is there anyone who can claim they have not any

Never will I concede to seek undue merit or favor
Ashamedly admit have engaged in lewd loose behavior

Granted imperfections yet implore you pause
Don't shun me for past transgressions only for current cause

Having bared my soul with candor pleading fresh new start
I declare my candidacy for consideration to win a true heart

New found character allowed to pursue a fine lass
Once not possible now good things came to pass

Confession is worthy if propriety is desired
Goal is achieved fine bride is acquired

by Dalward J DeBruzzi

Conundrum of Life

Tried to learn while yet a young child
What life was all about what it's intended to be

First attempt at comprehension found
beyond my powers
Elusive answer never materialized despite
intensive search countless hours

Years later an epiphany revealed you are
the revelation
My life was incomplete till you gave me
stimulation

With grave impassioned thought if I leave
this life today
With passion can say loved you unselfishly
every day

Know repeatedly went extra mile for you
My devotion and love altruistic and true

My feelings merely reflections your devotion to me
Willing consideration for each other was the key

Over the years when I held you my eyes wet with tear
My heart beat furiously rapidly only because of you dear

As my autumn song nears its final breath
My greed wants more after life and death

As in life you maintained entertained with love and care
We had it ideal will sustain the idyllic eternally share

by Dalward J DeBruzzi

Courageous Rebel

We are losing our courageous rebel leader
to be hung for all to see
King decreed he must adorn the infamous
hanging tree

His courage in resistance was daring to
follow
Led his armies not followed them to deliver
counterblow

He was ferocious in battle with daring skill
With resigned assignation to find a way to
kill

When arrested our leader caused many yet
to tremble in fear
His courage was heartening observed his
good cheer in incarceration
Let these men go or I'll see you in
damnation

He was a man among men in our rough band
Seen him scatter a phalanx of men by his
lone hand

Took him alone in the pub but the cost was high
They marched him in midst of upraised spears to die

He won't be mentioned in any book by tyrants or kings
No martyrs will be publicized whose bravery sings

He was a victim of censored deactivated scribes
Ignoring the popular supportive polls with bribes

The feast celebrating his coming demise
Was sumptuous, festive but then the surprise

We stormed the prison tower rescued our savior
Instructed us no matter he is our leader in favor

He is brave honorable a man you trust
With victory or defeat payment in lives is a must

by Dalward J DeBruzzi

Did We Know?

Kisses the key to dichotomous choice
pleasure or sin
My coveted one swears she's with joy longing
within

In helpless condition now court wench for
wife
Hope not hasty pursuing mate for life

I love thee for those eyes your hair
Those rosy cheeks ruby lips, lovely white
teeth so fair

Prudent pious orderly behavior sharing our
future a plus
Plans to tarry and not marry cause grief
pain and fuss

Melting our souls thus into one
Lasting happiness and joys did begun

**With tender loving words he did lovingly
eager greet
Tasting her lips repeatedly soft and sweet**

**Each ardent encounter as superb as the
past
The surest assurance that our glorious
union will last**

by Dalward J DeBruzzi

Enchantment

When first you burst upon my view you gave
me jolting galvanic start
Warmed my soaring passion my racing
throbbing heart

Thought of tardy absence leaves me coming
fast apart
Overwhelmed by your goodness grace and
polished art

The shower of affection you rain on me
generously favors delicious dreams
Sustenance and nutrition from thy radiance
teems
Your loveliness enhanced with gracious
humility beams

Traveled as mortals then mystics together
in harmony
With bountiful compassion love's devotion
our destiny

To enjoy the present and into eternity
Is the ultimate gravitation to lasting
harmony

by Dalward J DeBruzzi

End of Pleasant Journey

My final mortal day is closing as night falls
dark
No longer bright sunshine spaces unlit and
stark

Voices now beckoning from remote unknown
places
My feet treading towards paths unknown
new graces

My fabric of life now diaphanous frail and in
decay
Leaving thou who made my life so rich now
fading away

Alas dear one I fear I cannot stay
Oh true companion Oh true love Oh partner
ever mine

Be close to me though all else from me is
slowly drifting
Your past gifts and present allied memory
uplifting

Knowing you're with me to comfort succor and behold
Smoothes my unfamiliar journey towards a pious fold

Dismisses anxiety fear of unknown things random
Will wait till you rejoin me then restore our tandem

by Dalward J DeBruzzi

Eternal Life

First a glowing epitaph then long rambling
glowing verse
Now procession led by long shiny black
solemn hearse

Whether funeral presided over by rabbi, a
man or priest
Assured hear words of praise compassion a
literary feast

What is the hypocrisy attached to scene we
dread
Does death make mockery exploiting untruth
about the dead

Is honesty more compatible with truth or
religion?
Not saying the deceased was scoundrel, but
exuding contagion

Unvarnished truth was a rogue, lambrick, and
a crook
No person was immune to his vices of this
foul rook

Nay dishonorable to accurately assess faults of demised
So we refrain, restrain not wishing occasion to be compromised

We distort the truth with euphemisms with a stretch
Concealing not admitting the goner was a wretch

by Dalward J DeBruzzi

Faithless

Marie was it because I briefly stayed away?
Only a short time but you still wantonly did stray

No more will I rely on fickle lovely maidenly charms
Dreaming wrapped affectionately in your arms

Aghast frustrated deceived lover pitiful sorry fool
Foul detestable dissemblers of true hearts cause enamored to sadly drool

Desirable sweet lass in disguise with mock sincerity
Deficient in character bankrupt with charity

Wise one's detect thy wanton devouring reach
Through guilt and glare fair to say no proper adequate speech

Unmoved by conscience immune to remorse
Unwilling party to inaccurate discourse

Your false excuse to wander and betray
Inadequate camouflage to justify urge to stray

My good fortune was discovering your untrue bent
In time to avoid disaster message heaven sent

by Dalward J DeBruzzi

Fallen Angel

No medicine for thy grief I care to procure
Lost love for you must bravely endure

Pleading for forgiveness on mute ears fall
Infidelity fractured my heart not yours at all

You forsaked my trust and faith alas no more tries
Worshiped you once nevermore now totally heart denies

You blunted my passion in treacherous cruel fashion
Without true heart no sincere devout passion

I cringe from wounded spirit fierce and bold
Memory of betrayal grievous pain to behold

Dreamy eye tender thoughtful brow
Heart beating untrue where is it now

Once captivated heart compatible in kind
Banished from memory purged distastefully dined

Fallen Goddess exposed dethroned with
honor shorn
No remorse can I conjure for unfaithful one I
mourn

by Dalward J DeBruzzi

Fate

As I was idly walking I overheard a maiden talking
Prim, gracious, petite I succumbed to gawking

No! No! She cried forebode I know not your portent
Beware your tepid interest avoid status of old maid bent

Oh! That is sad indeed and unjust impetuous as well
She was my queen in my aroused heart she did dwell

Clasping her waist I stole a kiss in haste
Shocked she sputtered forsooth beware am chaste

With sweet comments made her cheeks glow new thoughts sprouted
In confusion the make up, rouge came down resistance flouted

All at once with sincere logic and appeal I
won her love
We were Adonis and Aphrodite soaring the
heavens above

by Dalward J DeBruzzi

Finding Heaven

Love is potent a thing of great force
Chemistry the catalyst which powers its
source

When absent a vacuous tormenting pain
cannot endure
Corrections meliorations supplications no
known cure

Subtle things noticed for love we engage
and conspire
Searching seeking for elusive tender love
raging fire

She is wrapped in his arms with head on his
chest
Moaning and sighing you may guess the rest

by Dalward J DeBruzzi

Flight Diet

Sweet corn, peas and pork chop ready for flight
Excited calm slightly flushed turning white

Take off jolting rumble in stomach groaned
Steep take off sharp ascent held stomach moaned

Light headed woozy dizzy and nauseous too
Doubtful good idea on the diet ingested then flew

Descent for landing inflicted mounting distress
Stomach revolting gave way caused real mess

Sweet corn, peas and chop not sure good prep for a flight
Will change pre-flight diet to liquids hoping I'm right

by Dalward J DeBruzzi

Genetic Mysteries

Oh unexpected misery dire to be borne
We laugh at the presence of genes bitter
scorn

Rejection kindles within us raving thirst
To prove personage of worth decry genetic
curse

The birthright of all beings acquire
knowledge and power
No restrictions limitations from challenge
nare cower

All men mortal alas not all with humanity
Distinctions narrow falsity defying sanity

Genetics indicator but not accurate with
exclusions
Vibrant world unbridled ambition hopeful
conclusions

Our soaring misery of non promising birth
Decrying gloomy prediction encourages
cynical mirth

From unfavorable prediction and faith self worth grew
Diligence enterprise serious effort work directs pursuits
Will subvert dire origin and bear delicious fruits

by Dalward J DeBruzzi

Grievance

Women may grieve deplore abhor loss of
chastity
When hope remedy gone no recovery of
probity

Tis a piercing dart from Cupid's admonitive
heart
Ere the circumstance suits the part

There was no blatant carnal motive devoid
of grace
Only innocent tender love unfolding
innocently at dignified pace

As many living and breathing know they
have an untapped need
With warm normal hearts the temptation to
scant decorum may exceed

Yet in their sweetness of failed prudity is
not seeking happiness worthy indeed
Caution pause do not self despair thy motive
was noble took courage reach and
proceed

No lamentation needed or shame to brave
the unknown
More often than not works out well take the
throne

Thousands misstep in reaching for perfect
harmony
Common temporary phase must sail through
it with dignity and hints of matrimony

Enough to see ransomed many millennium
in time and thought without rancor
Who struggled for redemption despite minor
detour

Then with discovery am now stronger, wiser
and secure
Erred innocently but better in reassembled
character
She lived wondrous young with vitality
regrouped with new endeavor

That's not their only treasure give them
praise
Honor them all despite their current phase

by Dalward J DeBruzzi

Happy Ending

Delays in love cruelly crucify the heart
It's no balm to play lost love's part

Clasped in the arms of the woman I love
While she coo's at me like a melodious dove

When she was young not yet twenty had suitors many
With pious moral dignity would not sport with any

I used the wings of love and to her I flew
Sighed kissed her hand no hesitation or rejection I knew

She blushingly begged I should grant her more
For us both as we stared there stood Cupid at the door

She drew herself nigh to me gently touched my face
Engulfed in raging fire no inhibition nary a trace

We faced each other without a blush
The things that developed were not in rush

We waited to caress be graced and blest
Now as her husband I render lawful
pleasure do my best

by Dalward J DeBruzzi

Heartbreak

I saw her beautiful face pink with blushing grace
In the tender ceremony watched betrothed embrace

Saintly sight lovely can inflict deep pain
Inherent shame burdensome indeed ever so vain

Watched coveted one in glorious joy inflicting distress
She moved further away in distance and no redress

I was defeated as a suitor formerly her devoted pursuer
Crawled in defeat while ego destroyed

Heart never truer remnants of morale salvaged and buoyed
Years later aided by random vicissitudes my long dreamed of goddess was pursuable in mid-song

Years back the beauty of the bride was
blushing stunning
Now older but mine eyes see only happiness
over running

As a raging roaring flame or a great fever
which we now share together
We vow eternal existence bond never to
sever

Waiting with patience deep love will endure
when ripened
God I thank so profoundly our future now
brightened

by Dalward J DeBruzzi

I Don't Know

Kisses the key to dichotomous choice
pleasure or sin
My coveted one swears she's with joy
longing within

In helpless condition now court wench for
wife
Hope not hasty pursuing mate for wife

I love thee for those eyes your hair
Those rosy cheeks ruby lips, lovely white
teeth so fair

Prudent pious orderly behavior a favorable
plus-
For plans to tarry and not marry cause grief
pain and fuss

Melting our souls thus into one
Lasting happiness and joys have begun

**With tender loving words she did lovingly
eager greet
Pressing her lips repeatedly soft and sweet**

**Each ardent encounter as superb as the
past
The surest insurance that our glorious union
will last**

by Dalward J DeBruzzi

Individuality

There are some who borrow and some who lend
Some who stand firm and some who bend
Some who love humanity and some engage in inanity

There those who don't fit in molds, categories or slots
A group called the haves and some called the have nots

One class is obese the other anorexian can't eat
To belong to the best class part luck no feat

There are those who are weaponless and those weaponed
Neither category necessarily sought after or beckoned

Everyone similar or quite different in ways
Diversity normal not a singular faze

Traits not drastically different we hope
But likeness not necessary to successfully cope

by Dalward J DeBruzzi

Insatiable Appetite

Frustrated young man lacked a mate
Discovered heart throb wonderful fate

Hugged kissed sweet talked soothed her no
action
But little else he did to subdue her passion

She angrily objected! Let this hugging
kissing end!
Is this all this relationship can portend?

Try to do better she cried the other is missing
Your behavior suits a mother or sister to be
kissing

A lover's diet I wish to be served not the
other
It seems you've no wish and it's a hungering
bother

All of one thing a loathing will bring
Play my tune and for you I'll sing

Young man heard the plea and did promptly conspire
Subdued the fire and met the torrid desire

Young man and mate now in conjugal contentment
Matrimony blissful fulfilled no longer resentment

by Dalward J DeBruzzi

Intrusion

I am Mr. Moon 293 million miles from earth
I'm far away it was my protection now my
dearth

My circumference is 6786 miles mind my
own affairs
Then one day aliens appeared in pairs

They abused me, scratched me, stepped on
me ripped some of me up
Left a flag on me, deep foot prints then
disappeared abrupt
Aliens appeared again and again am worried
they'll corrupt

Greater fear of all I can say
On one of these visits they may decide to
stay

by Dalward J DeBruzzi

It Was Worth It

My forbears were captured brought on ships
in chains
Brutalized whipped as slaves in labored pains

Struggled suffered cause taken up by
sympathetic supporters

Many lost their lives aiding my cause for
release
Battles raged violently for slavery to surcease

Above it all I can emphatically say
For me and mine it was worth it today

We enjoy schools, opportunities, the sky's
the limit
Have senators, congressman doctors lawyers
must admit

Gifts my kids and I enjoy on the shoulders of
others
Thanks expressed here no way adequate as
what thanks covers

Can sincerely encourage my kids to aspire
for unbridled goals
Even consider running for president or
mayor no confining molds

Price not paid by me, but my forebears with
exigency
Blessings are mine and thy by ancestral
blood and legacy

How fortunate am I and mine to live in this
plethora of opportunity
Heavens smiled on us now must pursue
continuity

by Dalward J DeBruzzi

Memories

Not a day expires when your memory is
unkind
I treasure the pictures that form in my mind

I can gyrate and swim in luxury in any one
single feature of your revered face
Remembrances are treasures in my heart's
coveted place

Slender nose so elegantly narrow with
proper tilt
Its beauty suggests heavenly built

Sunshine warm and shining visions when
just sitting
Your symmetrical pose in itself most
refreshing and fitting

Tho recall is not all picturesque there is
more to say
Things love made doing for each other in
every way

Create need to recall past with memories sweet
With tender recall comes surge of emotional heart beat

Simulated vicarious repeats of acts once done
Way of reliving sacrosanct acts from memory anon

Past experiences once embraced so zealously with zeal
Can revive at will for repeated pleasure as real

Charitable feature memory phenomenon is filter effects
It accents the good and subverts and rejects

My treasure to expend whenever I choose is soothing
Memories revived tender emotions oozing

When one is blessed with mother lode of
deep affection
With treasure trove of past things recorded
with selection

No need only rejoice nothing ever lost in
devoted felicity
Two as one in long years of complicity
Noble pure free of all duplicity

by Dalward J DeBruzzi

Miscalling

Each night my discomfort and accompanying pain
Malady accenting relief in vain

Despite great effort couldn't handle the mission
My resolve restrained am in remission

Felt anointed and selected
As many others were rejected

Pledged myself to an order to serve oath to celibacy
Found to comply needed to abandon all delicacy

Young healthful body yearns aches for outlet without censure
Fought hard banished thoughts of carnal pleasure
Tried adjustments self gratification can't resist the pressure

Went to mother superior for counsel and advice
Suggested more prayer and kneeling said it would suffice

Found calling of my body stronger than oath to sacrifice for celibacy
My call grew weak abandoned the novitiate and training
Unrealistic against biological compelling urging straining

Preserved my integrity to myself of identity
Did not promise what couldn't perform with integrity

Escaped life of purgatory guilt unfulfilled satisfaction
Ostensibly pious, while seeking illicit gratification

With thousands of priests under indictment and in jail
My decision seems sagacious and correct common sense did prevail

Once considering living against basic natural law
Was impractical to consider my reasoning a flaw

Innocent girls and decent young men should resist fiats
That demand celibacy confine it to chit chats

by Dalward J DeBruzzi

My Autobiography

I live in a nice house not so old
To survive I must live dangerously and be daring and bold

I am careful and wait until it's dark to come out
To be seen in daylight might cause a shout

Only when it's dark do I emerge at all
For I must eat to live life is a pall

I scavenge on floors, counters for packages to gnaw into
Careful to avoid poisons, traps is hard to do

So far I've been fortunate not my siblings laid flat
One ate what he thought was candy one caught in trap

Today is my birthday found a chocolate chip cookie
Gorged myself what! felt groggy, dizzy

Couldn't see too well was unsuspicious took
another bite or two
My mistake was fatal it was that last chew

Came to the conclusion my presence was
unappreciated in the house
But I lived it up long time free rent and food
the due of a mouse

by Dalward J DeBruzzi

My Regret

My stupidity is pride and false ego increased
We who assume the most know the least

When ages later revelation reveals this
misguided notion
By then damage, bruised feelings, bruised
relationships in motion

No contrition orated or 2nd chance will
erase the ruin and destruction of lives
from malfunction
Accepting castigation causes bitter tastes
from compunction

Hardest chore is to recognize own massive
error with great reluctance

We're only what we think we are not in true
perspective
To correct the vague vision requires being
selective

Admissions of faults curbing inflated ego
Two feet now on ground hyperblia in veto

by Dalward J DeBruzzi

No Ceilings Please

Oh unexpected misery dire to be borne
We laugh at predictive genes generate
bitter scorn

Predictive mediocrity kindles rebellious
raving thirst
Prove personage of worth decries negative
genetics curse

Beings acquire knowledge ambition hope
never sour
No restrictions limitations from the challenge
nare cower

Mortals alas some inadequately supplied in
humanity
Favored prospects a genetic anomaly an
amenity

No deterrence from desire to improve fend
off exclusion
The distinction no falsity imposes distorted
false illusion

Our soaring misery of dire predicted birth
Destroying given ceilings encourages cynical mirth

Lesson learned refuse limitations imposed on you
Push to the limit all prospects even if only a few

Diligence enterprise serious goals and pursuits
Can subvert dire prophecies and bear delicious fruits

by Dalward J DeBruzzi

Not Flashy but Steady

I am a draft horse, huge heavy not fleet of foot
Not sleek with smooth lines, form style or cute

While not pretty by equestrian standards of comparison
My power strength endurance unmatched in application

Can pull heavy drays, plows, hay wagons discs too
Beer keg loads, ice or milk is easy for me to do

Haven't the fine lines of a thoroughbred of beauteous design
I'd win no races but do the heavy work in rapid time

**Helped win the West pulling Conestoga
wagons for pioneers
Went slowly but when needed circling
galloped apace**

**Ignored attacking Indians running alongside
Never deterred from duty or failed to abide**

**My ancestors were mounts for King Arthur
and knights of old
Why even served Charlemagne, Roland and
Oliver and others too numerous to be
told
Down through history I pranced proud and
bold**

**I may not be pretty but I was favored always
ready
A serviceable horse powerful and steady**

by Dalward J DeBruzzi

Nothing

She wallowed in disdained trodden path
Away from chaste admirable things incurring wrath

A soiled maiden no praise or esteem nary one voice
None did she love no option or choice

She lived in murky shadows unseen by pious eyes
No one really knew her none cared or uttered cries

She withdrew receded ceased to exist
No tear sorrow lament not expressed did not persist

Cold lonely desolate grave unremembered
Unmissed unmourned all memory dismembered

A tragic end to profligate spurious existence
failure to mend
How wasteful of life some extravagantly
expend

by Dalward J DeBruzzi

Permanent Temple

I was a mountain man alone isolated no
company, in solitude
No people, no towns, villages, farms only
my entrenched rectitude

Desire to be protective interlopers I exclude
My story is simple man seeking access to a
kingdom whose vastness a virginal
essence free of social servitude

Free space without social restraint or intense
endeavor
Companions are deer, moose, elk, and beaver
Their lack of deceit makes me a believer

Glory in the freedom and the adventure of
being the first
Important to me like slaking a craving thirst

My need for new adventure a gnawing need
Seeking the new the unexplored is my diet
indeed

Can't say I accomplished much but blazed few trails though
Was where no one else was friend or foe

Social constrictions crept in slowly tainting air
Starting running out of space no matter, too old to care

At the end of my long trail of free living I will declare
No one following me can live the free life I did not share

The taste of freedom in vast areas no longer there
Was the king of all I surveyed I did not share

Can never be had by any mortal ever again
I just had a gnawing insatiable appetite for roaming back then

I was just fortuitous and got there before others
Life was unique singular exciting but wanted no brothers

Was perfection, God-like in its virginal state
The beneficiary was me and it was great

by Dalward J DeBruzzi

Perseverance

When the pierced heart feels burning desire
Through throbbing veins courses searing fire

Feelings sublime lofty strains of virtues that
are thine
Provokes brighter higher beautifications with
aura divine

Pray draw near and you will hear
Things of soothing tenderness so dear

When icy bitter winter wind is blowing
vicious cold
Warm relationships enhance and do enfold

Profound true feelings withstand taxing trials
Existent neuralgia with vigorous denials

We had seen it plain in each other's eyes
Succumbed to fulfillment with contented
sighs

by Dalward J DeBruzzi

Pitfalls

Everyone knows what young lovers do
If mentioned would provoke a tight curfew

A virgin softly sighs a reservoir of wishes
and kisses
Dreaming of fulfillment and longing what
she misses

Her visionary Prince Charming has beauty
and charms
In her dreams vicariously enveloped in his
arms

Suggested thought lets kiss to lessen drought
and pain
And dare to dally with what I cannot name

She suffered remorse pray remove your hand
From wise behavior to risqué adventure she
spanned

What is it that makes thy sense and reasoning straying
Resistance resumed to avoid self betraying

No need to look rift with melancholia ashly pale
At altar with vows with Prince Charming did prevail

by Dalward J DeBruzzi

Planning

Summed up her assets set goals feasible
Surveyed her chances decided were seizable

Some are blessed with ability to discern
Others must struggle the hard way to learn

We must be ourselves not subject to a master
To concede independence and sovereignty
disaster

Who do you search for and wish to call
Do you hope he's young handsome and tall?

Fortuitous to find someone acceptable and
believable
After thorough vetting found someone
agreeable

Fond is the memory setting goals for selection
Wending a way achieving enjoying deep
affection

Conclusion patience and judgment sagely used is desired
Standards set for perimeters proper selection desired

by Dalivard J DeBruzzi

Prevailing Persistence

Poor young sailor came to court innocent
young maid
Her resistance surrendered and for him her
heart prayed

This comely duo agreed to wed in an agreed
time
If they could coax the mother into the proper
mind

Want of riches for gold was her insistence
to take
She resisted rejected denied approval to
forsake

Depressed couple with amorous kisses
parted that night
Defied disapproval young sailor commanded
her hearts delight
Years later with five lovely children everything
was right

Grandmother now repentant and remorseful
Desires to see grandchildren bringing gifts resourceful

Young couple forgiving and greets old crone
It's better forgive and forget than to keep picking a bone

by Dalward J DeBruzzi

Promises

If you desire to hear of a startling humorous
jest
Tarry a moment it will be expressed

Enticed my beloved to marry with promise
to make a big woman of her
First few years complaints of broken promises
and roles resounded disappointment
did occur

Tenth anniversary goal attained
In surprising fashion I shouldn't be blamed

Wife with acquired taste buds did run amok
Consumed food ravenously and grew without
luck
Promise to her now fulfilled in whole no
longer stuck

Stepped on a scale and lo and behold
She now weighed 400 pounds quite a load

My promise fulfilled to my beloved wife
Oath fulfilled of my bridal promise to her in life

Who can deny she is woman who's big in a way
Perhaps not in agreement with original idea but acceptable today

by Dalward J DeBruzzi

Proper Ending

My lovely entrancing Ramona is kind and
fair
She revels in my wit relieves my despair

Oh! Heaven one night exquisite pleasure
hope it will last
A proper reward for my persuasiveness of
the past

Nay! To prevent my Ramona's love turn to
hate
Will make amends defy me a tragic fate

Twas wondrous thing the first time we
closely met
Our mutual desire and passion did our future
set

Events birthed true love no room for fear
Found needed her rapturous eyes forever
near

My forceful assault made without scurrilous loves haste
Catapulted into a true love not in waste

Spacious room made for noble love in bloom
Dispelled all taint, rejection and gloom

She is in my full possession yet we desire more
She for full closure entreats me give o'er

We both sought path to happiness the ideal life
Love, dignity, peace, harmony, took her to wife

by Dalward J DeBruzzi

Reality

Have I snared you sweetheart only with show
If so confess it's important that I know

Am I a doting and fond besotted amorous malleable tool
A confused whining idolatrous laughable fool

Most strange it is a thing so sudden and intense
Blooming can be instantaneous yet make good sense

Murmurs of love it's melody so divine
When attraction forthright, honest, pure and in rhyme

Thus spoke the lass with warm kisses instilled
Projecting our happiness anticipating our future so rich so thrilled

Hallelujah! she is comprised of copious
varied charms
Came to me a pure bridal virgin into my eager
arms

by Dalward J DeBruzzi

Regrets

You say you love me do see it in your eye
Am ashamed to say I come up woefully shy
Incapable to return your true defined allures

Woman waits for me undisuadable and
defenseless
I reap the bounty with voracious greed how
senseless

Fortify my resistance refuse to listen to
entreaties
Insulated against temptation from aggressive
sweeties

Ah! My sweet adoring swain your heart now
bitter cold
No longer you plead and grovel at my feet
unabashed and bold

Thing you once offered so generous spiced
my living
Now confused addled in quandary about your
sudden reluctance in generous giving

Is it too late for us to probe and explore
together in review
My revised thinking urges many thoughts of
you with favor
Sweet life if discovered later sometimes
will savor

My new attitude and aroused interest can
make up for the time I wronged her
I hope I'm not too late for she and I too
confer
While we explore, find out if I'm the one
she'll prefer

by Dalward J DeBruzzi

Revulsion

The beauty I passionately did once adore
I now as much do reject and deplore

Tis money alone that lures the tainted
maiden
Rations meaningless affection dishonor
laden

Wayward maiden no pride and self respect
left
Then betrayed by sincere heart occupation
bereft

Whilst guilty senses washes away love finds
its way
She chanced permitted her heart rendered a
say
Enlightened stance and dazzled delight dawns
a new day

Raging mercenary fire now contained and subdued
Beauty discovers heart recovers noble self rescued

Love is free precious money can't buy
Conquers errant behavior brings happiness if you try

by Dalward J DeBruzzi

Scamp, Rogue, Scoundrel?

Shun, avoid, in situation to wed
Love to woo coax maidens to bed

Challenge to corrupt, defrock lasses of chastity
Using deception, guile, absent veracity

Went from lass to wench in continuous quest
Each dubious victory seems like the best

Asked one day prithee why don't you indulge in matrimony
Ashamed and embarrassed to admit hold it in acrimony

Too cowardly to commit to one special deserving person
Lacked the responsibility couldn't overcome natural aversion

Now in the twilight the regrets now accrue
Exhausted all credits all left now is residue

As the curtain slowly but surely lowers
Loneliness solitude only reward for one who cowers

No faithful mate did I meet true and take on
Are gracing someone else's presence with dedicated aplomb

Given the chance for circumspection in detailed review
Knowing what I know now and I were making my amorous debut

Would I amend my goals in another direction
To have faithful mate in final years shared affection

When running over list of past beauties in my grasp
Concede with frank admission the memories will last

Compared with others my life is in stark difference
Some need someone at hand while with me it's insignificance

Peace with myself and comfort of thought is present
A sought after condition makes everyone content

by Dalward J DeBruzzi

Self Destruction

She cheated then cruelly boisterously did laugh
Dishonest lover cans't be all honest less than half

My self respect and jealous eye rejects her tawdry past
Wench no cause not to expect ousting to ever not last

No relenting penance nor ease when you grieve
Act of treachery dismisses all chance of reprieve

Long were you indiscriminant who was in the saddle
Oblivious callus to infamy rumor or injurious prattle

Thy destiny sink into unstable ruin anon deep despair
You repented penalty bitter and harsh no longer care

**No longer love for thee why shoulds't you
still love me
Opportunity squandered we did tarry never
marry
My conscience untainted yours a heavy
burden to carry**

**Your ship has sailed from this once protected
port
Misery discontent earned reward when
morals abort**

by Dalward J DeBruzzi

Shameless

Evading obligations for gifts received is a practiced art
Scoundrels feeding on family, friends thinking it smart

If they receive a gift instead of saying thank you
Something be however trivial to complain is first clue

This in their mind dismisses the reciprocal action due
And artificially eliminates their responsible debt to you

If the gift comes by mail they deny it has arrived
It's a ploy that works but disgustedly contrived

Another technique in their sick bag of tricks
If received just don't call, don't communicate in any way
After lengthy amount of time resume speaking with no mention of the gift don't say

Unscrupulous family member using this form of theft
Unaware their mind fix anomalous of decency is bereft

This type of person has fooled themselves in denial
Refusing to acknowledge their faulty sense of being is on trial

Their foul behavior is nothing more than motivated by greed
It's just dishonorable hit and run a base philosophy indeed

If you're dealing with one in your family you're stuck
They go through life using you as a chicken to pluck

by Dalward J DeBruzzi

Surprise!

**Her face was heart shaped flawless sweet
ruby lips
Her slender arms tapering in harmony draws
raves and quips**

**Young firm sloping breasts tiny waist a
seraphim
Capacity for warmth affection no minimum**

**On the beach all eyes drink in her stunning
stances
Few can resist casting intensive lustful
glances**

**Shapely thighs sloping in tantalizing curves
Entrances weaves spell jangles nerves**

**Her athletic prowess graceful in movement
Precise actions and skill no room for
improvement**

Fell hopelessly deliriously in love deep
adoration
Proposed anxious to begin marital domicile
with expectation
Vows given wedding beautiful with great
exultation

Thrills from my bride expected her to be
versatile
On wedding night proved inadequate infantile

My perfect beauty lacking on our wedding
the plight
Great surprise with shock to discover blight

Was torpid, lethargic disinterested in amorous
delight
Like looking at prime filet impossible to bite

Is sadistic and frustrating destroying the
purview
Seeing beauty devoid of function is shocking
and won't do

I divorced with haste admitted the huge miscalculation
Extricated myself from vicarious castration

Learned lesson from surprise look in the package
See if it works and avoid wreckage

Detect amorous reluctance and resistance
Avoid impasse if it's regular in consistence

by Dalward J DeBruzzi

Sustenance

When immersed in thought with sessions of things past
Sighing, mournful regrets how things went fast

Nothing lasts forever think of thee without restraint
All regrets of losses only pleasant memories retained

I keep your letters a boost on a rainy gloomy day
Their touching tenderness warms me when I pray

With melancholy onset feeling dreary with dismay
Seek comfort quietly reading your letters each day

Together we wandered through life's complex maze
Old memories and new as seen through our gaze

Reminiscences cheer to the faint and weary
All this adds up to is past present now rosy future
Wealth of recall when rich and pleasing memories gives proper closure.

by Dalward J DeBruzzi

Symbiosis

Your joys toils love life I'll beseechingly share
Committed helpless captured hopefully you
care

Your irresistible charms too formidable to
resist
Heart afire absorbed consumed vanquished
does persist

Presence as my sweet loving bride my sole
mission
Quest for sublimity eliminates cause for
indecision

If common thought spirit desire shares
equanimity
Our future rosy expectant glorious sanguinity

Total absence of an undisciplined heart
Lends stability endurance a union destined
never to part

No deferment interruption will derail such a pact
A lifetime spent together confirms the tender fact

by Dalward J DeBruzzi

Thank You Heroes

Our police officers are heroes we revere them with awe
Each day they report to hazardous duty to enforce the law

Law man goes on duty not knowing if he will make it home alive that night
He performs this daily heroism to keep perpetrators in flight

Each moment at risk of sudden possible demise
From some twisted demented crazy who can kill by surprise

While in squad car riding patrol can be shot as bait
Serving a warrant killed by irate abused domestic mate

If he makes an error in a split second judgment he may be slain
If he does shoot and kills sometimes accused of lacking restraint then suffers disdain

Good citizens all over want protection from killers, rapists and robbers too
To be assured of safety in homes, on streets, L platforms
We should cooperate fully and earn the right, a good citizen conforms

To insure our sons and daughters safety first rule is tell them "obey instructions from police"
Many shootings are from disregarding police instructions
Remember they carry the law without compunctions

GOD BLESS AND KEEP OUR OFFICERS SAFE!
GOD BLESS AND KEEP OUR CITIZENS SAFE!

by Dalward J DeBruzzi

The Awakening

There lived a farmer's daughter upon a
pleasant green
Many guesses of age were made but ere
was sixteen

With skin of startling white and presence to
stun an eye
The suitors were many with proposals they
did try

Land owners, doctors, men of looks and
means she did decry
Rejected refused declined all overtures
firmly did deny

With confusion puzzlement to herself she
had no clue why
None of her suitors appealed to her she did
sadly sigh

On a sunny fresh spring day she met Miss
Molly McGrew
Her answer came to her and now as she
discovered her nature true

by Dalward J DeBruzzi

The Bursted Bubble

She reclined in her silken bed
An I was present and did lay by
No cover or garments about her spread
No modesty left without wraps had I
Delirious with mad delight threw my arms about her
But nay twas a shock dreamy fantasy fugacious only
Reality sobered compelled exist with wishes not lonely
Awoke to my dreamy vague fantasy in confusion
As reality crushed me and scattered my illusion
Though stark disappointed and downcast am I
Longing for a repeat would be nice wish I'll try

by Dalward J DeBruzzi

The Game

When she was young under twenty had
suitors many
With pious modesty dignity desisted sporting
with any

Married women may take or leave
Whatever they chose to refuse or receive

But maidens are restricted to yes or no
It seems unfair but this is so

They try to be witty effervescent and smile
Selectively use artifices in efforts to beguile

Maiden successful when she attracts the
right beau
Can nestle in the arms of betrothed affection
can flow

Hath surrendered her treasures cooing
softly as a dove
Wedding vows echoed with blessing from
above

Enfranchised hands caress explore with license
All actions now approved in delightful essence
Who's love she has, by winning his heart

In realm of approvement we enjoy each tender caress
Loves Elysium added anointed enriching each other we possess

by Dalward J DeBruzzi

The Rescue

A rosy apple cheeked frivolous unhappy lass
With caustic sneer mourned no swain came
to pass

Along came rustic hearty lad a mind to gain
her favor
With clever wanton thought sought her love
to savor

His tender arms around her body entwined
She pleaded behavior with effort to remain
refined

Such display of affection the bonnie lass
espied
Ingredients in motion hints can I be a bride

Hearty rustic youth queried fair lass how
thee fare
Our clandestine pleasure so startling forsooth
Truth in admission satisfied my sweet tooth

What troubles thee said she I fear I'm a maid in grief
A deep grievous wound festering no possible relief

Oh he replied that's all I'll take you for wife gentle maid
Pious blessing approval your stature no one can abrade

by Dalward J DeBruzzi

The Revolt

Naughty Rhonda now you've cruel become
I swear you most unjustly to unkindness
have succumb

Only asked for sampling taste
What you denied me slowly then in haste

A kiss but with a coquettish disdain
You observed my sighings and profound
pain

Not willing or eager to be kissed rebuffed
me with frown
Undeterred I slyly willfully loosed your
clinging gown

Begged you to relent and grant the meanest
joy
Saw denial in eye cried your just engaging
another ploy

I deplore nauseous naughty behavior crude and bold
Tis well said since I'm firmly denied now indifferent and cold

Naughty Rhonda coy shrewd and complex
Used artifices in variety to tease and vex

Teasing without sincerity she played coy
Exhausting patience using me like a toy

Naughty Rhonda no longer holds my interest
Immature faithless behavior she did display
From this I declined and drew away.

Skirmishes and tug of war then ran its course
Probing experimenting gave way to amorous force

The campaign is over with indistinct conclusion
Did I gain worthy wife or take on confusion?

by Dalward J DeBruzzi

The Shiny Black Crow

The trim shiny black crow up on the tall oak tree
Swiveling his head around to see what he could see

Perched on the highest bough with graceful ease
Enjoying the refreshing wafting breeze

Left his perch soared away how far have you gone today
Distance traveled on wings so strong fluttering in play

He sought far places across the vast grey bleak sky
No radar guide only instinct desire to soar and fly
Flapped oer the busy city speeding through the sky

Stacks belching smoke dotting things in soot
Starting acrobatics trying to be cute

Now cavorting in loops and crazy figures in the waning light
Pleasing conclusion to sightseeing flight

by Dalward J DeBruzzi

The Tramp Steamer

Leaving Japan, China, Java and Singapore
with loaded hold
The tramp cargo ship returns, when trading
goods are sold

Out of San Francisco with wheat, corn and
rye
Destined for Philippines with food they
require in steamer they did hire

Owners advised to refit and repair tramp
steamer its turn
Ignored advice wanted more profit to earn

With load of coconuts, copra and pineapple
heading to Peru to unload at the Lima
port quay
Loading copper and zinc then anchoring in
Boston Bay

Taking on fuel and provisions, cargo of
potatoes, textiles
Sailed toward Iceland encountered sea
trials

Arctic storm of ferocity and force assaulted the tramp steamer
Battered by winds, waves forty feet high
Unfavored by luck no success though they try

Tramp steamer went down with all hands fighting
King Triton delivered a crushing blow upon sighting

Tramp Steamer and men lost to ocean blue and vast
If reasonable and prudent would have continued to succeed

by Dalward J DeBruzzi

The Widow

The widow was fair and lovely in the quaint small town
Many strove to have her as a jewel in their crown

Her stunning golden tresses like shining gold
Sent suitors blood racing imbuing them daring bold

They came on awooing eagerly pursuing still
Were rebuffed and refuted by her strong prevailing will

Her words sweet as honey which made her suitors throng
Poised reserved composed said you didn't sing my song

She dismissed state and pomp but in tandem very sweet
Romance of widow and Adonis glorious grandly emerge
Losers for hand of Widow Blair lost heated prior urge

Adonis completely happy but informed by widow new
Neglected to tell you have seven children in my crew

by Dalward J DeBruzzi

The Wish

Pray! Yes! I could love deeply if I could find
A maiden fair that suits my mind

Whom free from ego, no crave for riches
could not alter
Express loyalty and passion without
hesitation or falter

Did love me for myself and not mine
Possessed gentle character steady noble
and fine

If such a one exists and perchance I find
She's the maiden for me she suits my mind

by Dalward J DeBruzzi

There's Nothing Wrong with You

I look normal, not talented, not dumb people
don't seem to seek me out
Others seem to have no trouble enjoy friends
about

Why no one seems to look my way engage
me first?
You are mistaken and foolish to think you're
the only one with a social thirst

You have not used trial and error to develop
techniques to foster friends
Won't happen without experimentation to
create interest and trends

First attempt should be greet cheerfully
when opportunity arises
Believe it being greeted first are pleasant
surprises

Learn to say pleasant things that please no end
Compliments soothe oil the path to a speaking friend

Ask for no commitments it's much too soon
Trend slowly a step at a time is a pleasing tune

Everyone without knowing it feels their way along
Remember a person will respond if approach is impersonal but continuously repeat the song

Treat each person special in what they say and do
Show interest in family kids some friends will accrue

You may not get proper reaction initially don't despair
Happens to everyone just hang in there

Response to joviality with discretion and consistency
Will cure your incorrect thought of your deficiency

No matter who you are if out reach with warmth and charm
Your life with enrich you may bet the farm

by Dalward J DeBruzzi

Treasure of Childhood

In early midsummer children are happy and glad
Though they're smaller they're surely not sad
They enjoy many things adults fail to appreciate

In our innocence and naiveté we are sometimes coy
Young minds can get pleasure from a simple toy
Untainted by mature attitudes unexposed by excess only joy

Unbridled pleasure is a child's providential state
Unaffected by mature prejudices, a fortuitous fate

The crime of growing up too fast is a child's due
Their idyllic state of innocence a debt that will accrue

Guard, protect, nourish the childish phase
It's the most valued time of a youngster's
world with merit and praise

by Dalward J DeBruzzi

Ubiquitous Egalitarian

Summoning all people of every creed religion and race
All included with outstretched arms warm embrace

Brotherhood of egalitarianism warm heart and peace
Oath includes pietism but chauvinism must cease

Wanton waste destruction cost prosperity and lives
Sincerity altruism endurable worthwhile and survives

Everyone deserves considerate treatment not like a fool
Gentility the opportunity to attend school

Find opportunity to help fellow man
This is the noblest activity if you can

Camaraderie and support is all about giving a helping hand
Requires feeling compassion magnanimous how grand

Not confusing in the least nor at anon complex
It's just about decency and proper humane reflex

by Dalward J DeBruzzi

Uncut Jewel

Poor am I but a plain and harmless maid
In most eyes my comeliness would gently
from view fade

Not true your gifts not visible, gaudy or cheap
Is not loyalty, truth, goodness worthy harvest
to reap?

Hidden sterling qualities makes a loving
adored bride
Camouflaged qualities are easy to hide

Seized her warm consenting ardor begging
for her hand
Her slender waist, tapering thighs heaving
breast so grand

Hidden gifts discovered revealed treasures
secreted
Forsook surface offering dug deeper was
well treated
Forsaked freedoms of single life took this
maid for my wife

by Dalward J DeBruzzi

Victim of the Game

Startled was I with sudden heat my heart
burning
Lifting a quizzical puzzling look for the fire
flourishing

One sunny day wrote her name upon the
sandy beach
The tide rolled in erased all letters despite
mute beseech

Resolved re-inscribed her name on the windy
sandy shore
Persistent tide wind driven erased her name
as before

The seed ye sow sometimes another reaps
Wealth you accumulate another sometimes
takes

Life is fleeting nebulous at times uncertain
Merely fated progressive steps toward the
final curtain

On the obstacled journey do not dismay
It's the same for everyone though you're
proper and pray

If philosophy proper will enjoy each day and
dawn
Despite irritants, impediments, love, living,
desirable future favorably drawn

by Dalward J DeBruzzi

Vulnerable

Delays when in love crucify the heart
It's no balm or comfort to play lost love's part

Abandoning impatience with vivacity
Lessons the achy pains of prolonged travesty

Embraced in each other's arms so natural
and right
Enjoying the pleasures created from a lover's
sight

Dwelling as one in our chosen town
Presented no enigma how best their love
might crown

And who can withstand the force of Sir
Cupid's desires
Resist fanning the sweet allure of rapturous
fires

Finally without faltering utterance to declare love and devotion
Lovers now fulfilled pain removed as if with lotion

by Dalward J DeBruzzi

Wasted

Mind and body uncoordinated and mismated.
Undergoes reverses injurious and hated

Intellectually cannot protect bodily charm
Her vulnerability unable to prevent harm

She resisted her best to preserve self worth
and esteem
Mismatched body and mind suffers reverses
bad dream

Lost the battle allowed treatment like cattle
ill fated
Led now far astray mind and body mismated

Mind inadequate to guard natural treasure
Steady involvement in monetary false
pleasure

Mind and body in concert can promote
decency self worth
Adopting standards of right no wrong a new
birth

Resisting mined paths of the lurking
lascivious throngs
Patiently adhering to good conduct in
harmonious songs

This faithfully applied will preserve and
protect body and soul
Yielding moral dividends the covetous goal

Natural progression to leading rich
wholesome life
Keeps the door open for good things maybe
even wife

by Dalward J DeBruzzi

Welfare Mother

I'm a welfare mother
Income I have no other

Can't live on the inadequate check
Our life is sparse miserable a wreck

My three kids just barely get enough to eat
Can you imagine my hurt and pain they never get a treat

Worry about my kids constantly drugs, drinking prostitution
Can't afford to move not enough money no solution

Pursued by an admirer didn't really want him
Needed a man to help with expenses so took 'em in

Went shopping for groceries mate baby sat
Molested my daughter out he went that was that

Things got worse now can't pay rent
Desperation forces things done to sadly repent

First time sold sexual favor sick and nauseous
Kids ate decently felt justified became incautious

Defamed activity earning good money
Our life though tainted was adequate and sunny

Things crashed was busted three times in a row
Lost kids to Child Welfare as unfit mother obsessed
In jail can't see children or visit them despondent and depressed

Tried my best to keep my family well and all together
Things choked me strangled me no livable weather

Six by eight is not an honorable cemetery plot
It's the best I could do as I hung myself
from the top

Avoid becoming a welfare recipient is
advised
Deck is stacked against surviving is
prophesied.

by Dalward J DeBruzzi

What Am?

Upon my bed my weary body lay
Without use or habit I do not pray

Yes I'm weak in many ways and unblest too
Around me strength and wisdom is not present
It's my debilitation scourge curse pain not lessened

Last night a first for me I prayed aloud
Felt refreshing surge above the fiendish crowd

Gradually sensed intolerable wrong
Those and what I scorned identified decent and strong
Such grief I have absorbed transformed and prevailed

Faith trust goodness all counts with character to leaven
Lesson learned there is no short cut to heaven

by Dalward J DeBruzzi

What Goes Around
Comes Around

Who my sweetest one pays your tribute due
Tis me thy ardent adorant my heart is true

Only a poor sailor wishes to court pure innocent maiden
With unbridled passion devotion and love ever laden

He prevailed and her heart him did she adore
They were meant for union with happiness in store

This comely couple agreed to wed in proper time
When could persuade ambitious mother into proper mind
Impedance unless dowry greed wants what she can take

She objected denied would keep her daughter unwed
Unless rewarded no permission is what she said
The repressed depressed comely couple with amorous kisses

Disobeyed united without grace of wedlock
Ostracized by mother in state of shock

Years later with five lovely beautiful children all fair
Reaped happiness unbounded nothing to despair
Greedy mother remorseful lonely repenting anxious to repair

Wished to see daughter, grandchildren spouse feel family affection but broken connection
Regretted her errors and misjudgments of rejection

The comely happy couple with loving family tree
Responded, "Nay dear mother and desist it's not to be."

by Dalward J DeBruzzi

What Success?

All state in football excelled in everything
but studies
Never studied got good grades spent time
with buddies

Teachers helped all they could bent a lot of
rules
Accented the necessity to use educational
tools

I sensed my athletic skill was my ticket to
sail through
Graduated with outstanding grades my
payment from the U

Went to college on a full athletic scholarship
Was college hero on grid iron with my
leadership

Signed for big money on my way to riches
First year did ok lived it up life's vicissitudes
cause switches

Broke leg second game of year pain more
than can bear
First novocain, morphine, now desperate
cocaine
Now addicted can't play cut from team in
constant pain

Wife left me now homeless ruined and
shunned
Dazed ill health all happened to me stunned

Mistake made believed my own hyperbolic
absurdity
Should have taken college with serious
firmity

What success did I achieve for myself?
Not much of anything I fear broken and on
the shelf

by Dalward J DeBruzzi

Who Am I?

I am the spawn of water air and earth
Grow profusely in soil good and bad yet
despised dearth

I am attacked in corn rows with sharpened
hoes
Called undesirable names and issued killing
blows

Gardeners world over no race or ethnicity
like me
I'm hated vilified discriminated against all
agree

Pause now pose the question for your
explanation
What am I can you make an identification?

People say I'm obnoxious uninvited and
invasive
Some are unkind say I'm destructive and
evasive

**Just trying avoid sharp hoe clutching fingers
and hands
Intent upon my demise with no conscience
understand?**

**My existence risky mood despondent and
frayed
At every turn rejection vilification only
displayed**

**Since birth been hunted, said fair game for
eradication
It hasn't been easy being constant target
for elimination**

**Prospects mighty grim constantly under
observation
Other prospect submit to be plowed under
for aeration**

by Dalward J DeBruzzi

Who Me?

When the girls are falsely coy
Timorous in denial of knowledge and joy

Dismissing acquaintance with subjects they
would fain savor
Deceptive display fear when clandestinely
enjoys flavor

Naughty in thought the britches came down
fast
Desired dishonored thrills fleetingly last

From moment allowed covert lover inside
the door
He eagerly engages with ardency to tend
the store

With magnanimous latitude of lax behavior
Dismiss the transgression on grounds of
brief waiver

by Dalward J DeBruzzi

You Think You Know Me?

You think you know me but you don't
If you really did then thinking me nice you won't

You think my apparent sweetness sincere fixation
Subterfuge deception for gaining advantageous situation

You think you know me but you don't
My professed fidelity a fabrication of nimble thinking
Unsteady morals credibility sinking

You think you know me but you don't
Appearing kind considerate thrust for image of reliability
Designed to disarm pounce on staged vulnerability

My drinking substance abuse done in secrecy and stealth
False claims suggestions a lie of substantial wealth

You think you know me but you don't
You discovered my dark side completely at last
Refused to believe my oath to abandon the past

Completely exposed for treacherous scoundrel I am
Now cast out the door with no fanfare no sham

You think you know me you do and you by rejection
I see now you know me only too well by your defection

by Dalward J DeBruzzi

Young but Resolved

I'm shy timid young maiden courted by many
All sorts came to didn't want any

My gifts are my own I'll protect them still
Other lasses may do as they will

Handsome young man promised me all to be
his
Rejected his temptations not snared by this

Then a finance man with mountains of cash
Felt for sale corrupted no desire to be under
his lash

Along came a tailor with bolts of cloth in
hand
Swore fidelity placed himself at my
command

He emphasized the slit in my skirt above the
knee
Denied the offer of his to stitch it for me

Pursuit of me continued by dozens more
Rejected same pleas as many before

Young unsophisticated but did not respond
to a snap
Avoiding being a victim escaping a trap

My personal thing is my own I guard it still
My standards are high in my mind must fulfill

Other girls may do as they choose
My ardent wish they do not lose

My treasures are mine stand firm will try
Until chastely wed men may pass me by

by Dalward J DeBruzzi

CPSIA information can be obtained
at www.ICGtesting.com
Printed in the USA
FSHW021640260819
61423FS